LOVEFLAKES

Memories of Mirages

LOVEFLAKES

Memories of Mirages

VIBHA MALHOTRA

Illustrated by
Bharati Malhotra and Poonam Bhalla

Hawakal
PUBLISHERS
New Delhi | Calcutta

HAWAKAL
New Delhi | Calcutta

HAWAKAL PUBLISHERS
70 B/9 Amritpuri, East of Kailash, New Delhi 65
33/1/2 K B Sarani, Mall Road, Calcutta 80

Email info@hawakal.com
Website www.hawakal.com

Cover art by Bharati Malhotra
Cover designed by Bitan Chakraborty

First edition (paperback) April 2022

ISBN: 978-93-91431-59-4 (paperback)

Price: INR 450 | USD 16.99

To everyone who has ever made anyone feel loved.

In your light I learn how to love. ~ Rumi

THERE CAN BE NO GREATER TRUTH

a foreword to *Loveflakes*

As Vibha states in the first poem — *Love is cacophonous,* yet this collection offers a grounding for the concept and the experience of love. She defines her debut poetry collection herself by telling the reader —

Sometimes the poem you need hasn't yet been written.
Sometimes you need to write that poem yourself.

She moves on to write the poem and its many parts and pieces through the nuggets she gathers through *Loveflakes.* This collection is as comfortable being read as one powerful poem about love and its manifestations as it is being read in small bytes of calm and chaos and a pause settled sometimes.

You bring your calm. I'll get my chaos.
I might ruffle your surface a bit, but your calm will triumph.
My chaos will be calmed.

Vibha walks like a trapeze artist, the tight rope of love through these poems. She brings the bittersweet sensoria of love alive by moving in, out, and away from one type of love. She allows love to ask questions, probe beneath the surface of the tingled skin, stay centered, move through uncharted paths, and stay fearful and eager! This love undergoes metamorphosis through Vibha's pen, ultimately making its way ahead as she says in *Happy Ending* —

Instead, the scared me skirted the fire, and let our fingers entwine.
Now, we make our way ahead,
your hands exploring me,
your ravenous mouth whispering words, guiding flowers to bloom and birds to sing.

What I treasured most about this book is the impression of quiet as each poem shuffles across the page, trying not to disturb the reader's beating heart. Vibha stays patient with the poem and herself as she moves through words and white space. She has an intentional pace to each poem, a size that fits in a fist and then unfurls with each thoughtful word.

The illustrations accompanying each poem are poems themselves. They are the unspoken parts of the poem that the reader will linger and dwell with before moving on to the following verse. Finding the entry point from the poem to the illustration to the heart of each pair of poems/pictures is the most beautiful aspect of this collection.

By the time one finishes *Loveflakes*, one is drawn into a spell, and nothing else is left to uncover. As Vibha says in one of the poems — *there can be no greater truth.*

Loveflakes has been a pause for me — it nudged me to reacquaint with the layers of relationships and an unabashed humming of love.

7.83 Hz

I have listened to your heartbeat. There is
nothing else I need to hear. There can be no greater truth.

Congratulations on this sincere debut, Vibha, and may love always find you through poetry.

My tiny little poem for you as you scatter these love flakes into the universe —

fingerprints
your silence settling
into my shadows

Love, poetry, light!

Kashiana

Kashiana embodies the essence of her TEDx talk — Work as Worship into her everyday and she has just released her second full length collection, *Woman by the Door*, with Apprentice House Press.

Loveflakes

Love has been part of the conversation ever since humanity learnt how to communicate. So, you might think that everything that needed to be said has already been said. Yet many of us who brave love feel the need to share our experiences.

Loveflakes evolved mainly during the unpredictable times of the Covid-19 pandemic. The isolation forced us inward, yet it has never been more important to express what we feel. Moreover, the canvas of emotions has never been so stark — joy, sorrow, love, anger, loneliness, and belongingness all stood out with their vibrance turned up many notches.

Love unifies us with infinity. Only while we are in love do we have the opportunity to absorb answers to our existential questions. The cosmos holds these answers, and love is its DNA. I have deliberately stayed away from arranging these flakes into themes. Love is flaky, and so are love flakes. Experience this book as you would experience love. You never know what you will find on the next page.

Vibha Malhotra
March 2022
New Delhi

ACKNOWLEDGEMENTS

First of my thanks goes to my life partner Vijay who saw me go through all the emotional upheavals one does when committing one's words to paper and for the hours we spent brainstorming the title.

This book wouldn't have been possible without these beautiful couples. Without them, I wouldn't have known how to identify love. My parents, Santosh and Vijay Kumar Malhotra, parents-in-law Sumanlata and Baldev Chand Sharma, sister and brother-in-law Bharati Malhotra and Alok Sharma, sister-in-law and brother-in-law Indu and Umesh Sharma, and my friends Smita Dhall and Nandan Jha.

I would also like to thank my nephew and niece, Nishant and Urvi, who helped channel my inner child. Finally, I would like to acknowledge my friends Aakshi Chowdhary, Amrita Arora, Monica Saigal, Parul Gupta, and Poonam Bhalla, with whom I have often exchanged notes.

Thank you, Kiriti Sengupta, for keeping faith in me, and Bitan Chakraborty and Hawakal Publishers for helping me bring this book to light. Special thanks to Kashiana Singh for writing such a thoughtful foreword for *Loveflakes*. I am grateful that I ran into you while you were here for a short visit all those years ago.

CONTENTS

LOVEMAKING

We are cacophonous together.
But we will find our rhythm.
With patience and acceptance, one day,
we will dance to a symphony.

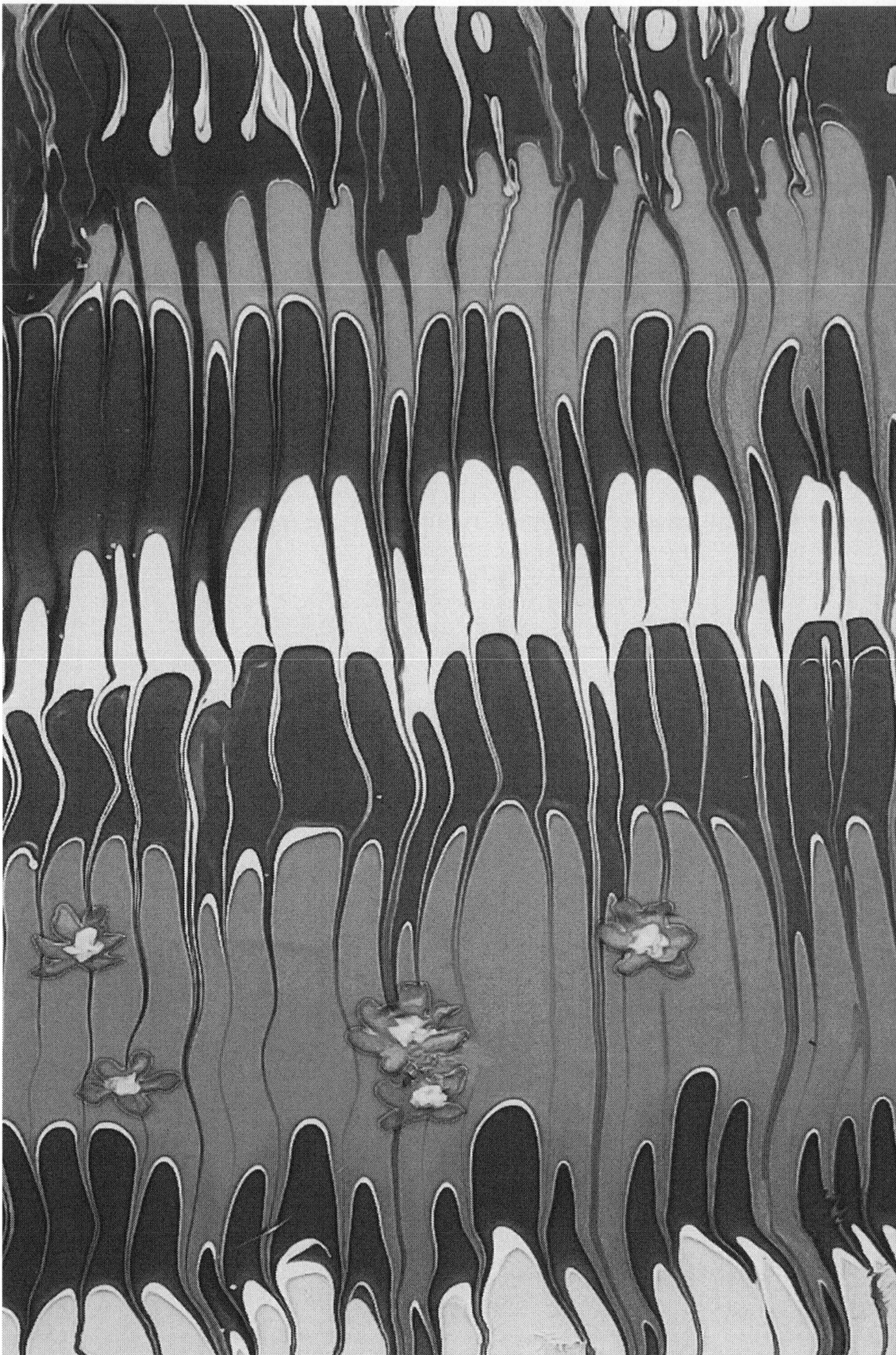

MY BEAUTIFUL HANDS

Remember when you made love to my hands?
You stroked the fingertips and buried your face
in my palms.
Never before had my hands felt so special.
I started seeing them in a whole new light.

TOUGH LOVE

Sometimes a 'No' is a bigger act of love than a 'Yes'.

CYCLE OF FEAR

I am afraid that my fear of losing you
will drive you away.
This makes me even more afraid.
This insecurity, it is a self-feeding fire.

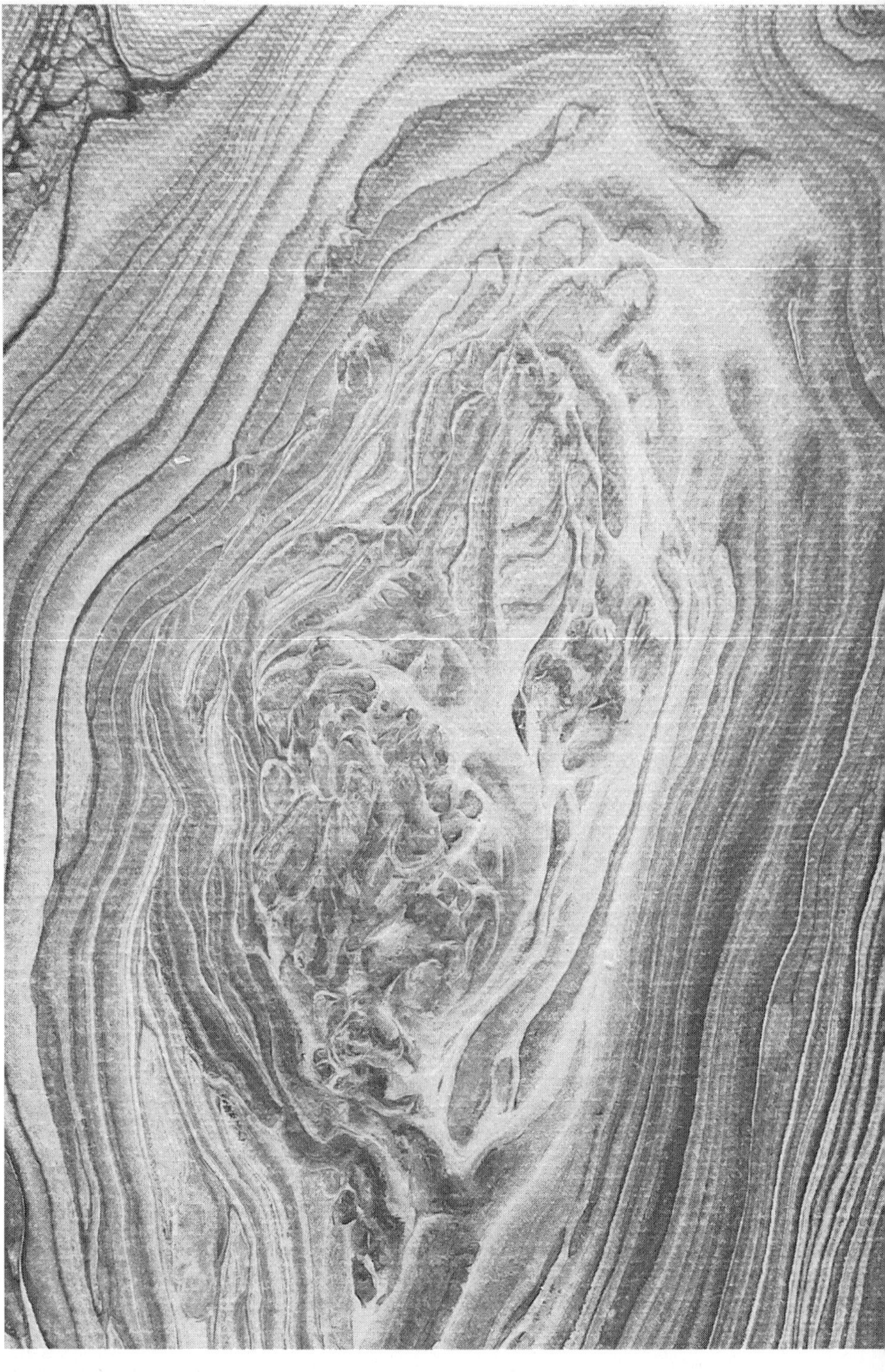

LOVERS

Look at those two
and their wrinkled, entwined hands
as they walk each other
from this street to that
from this shop to that
from this year to that…

THE ART OF DYING

We talk about moving on.
You say that after ten years,
maybe we will be able to look back at this
and laugh.
For me, this will always be that moment
when I had to extinguish a part of my soul,
so that the rest could survive.

LET'S NOT GET TOO USED TO WAITING

We have spent so many lives waiting
for each other.
When this wait ends,
will we even know how to be together?

DYNAMITE

You bring out the worst of my tempers.
But you also contain it
with your infinite tenderness.
You are the spark to my fuse
and water to my fire.

LOVEFLAKES

Sometimes the poem you need hasn't yet been written.
Sometimes you need to write that poem yourself.

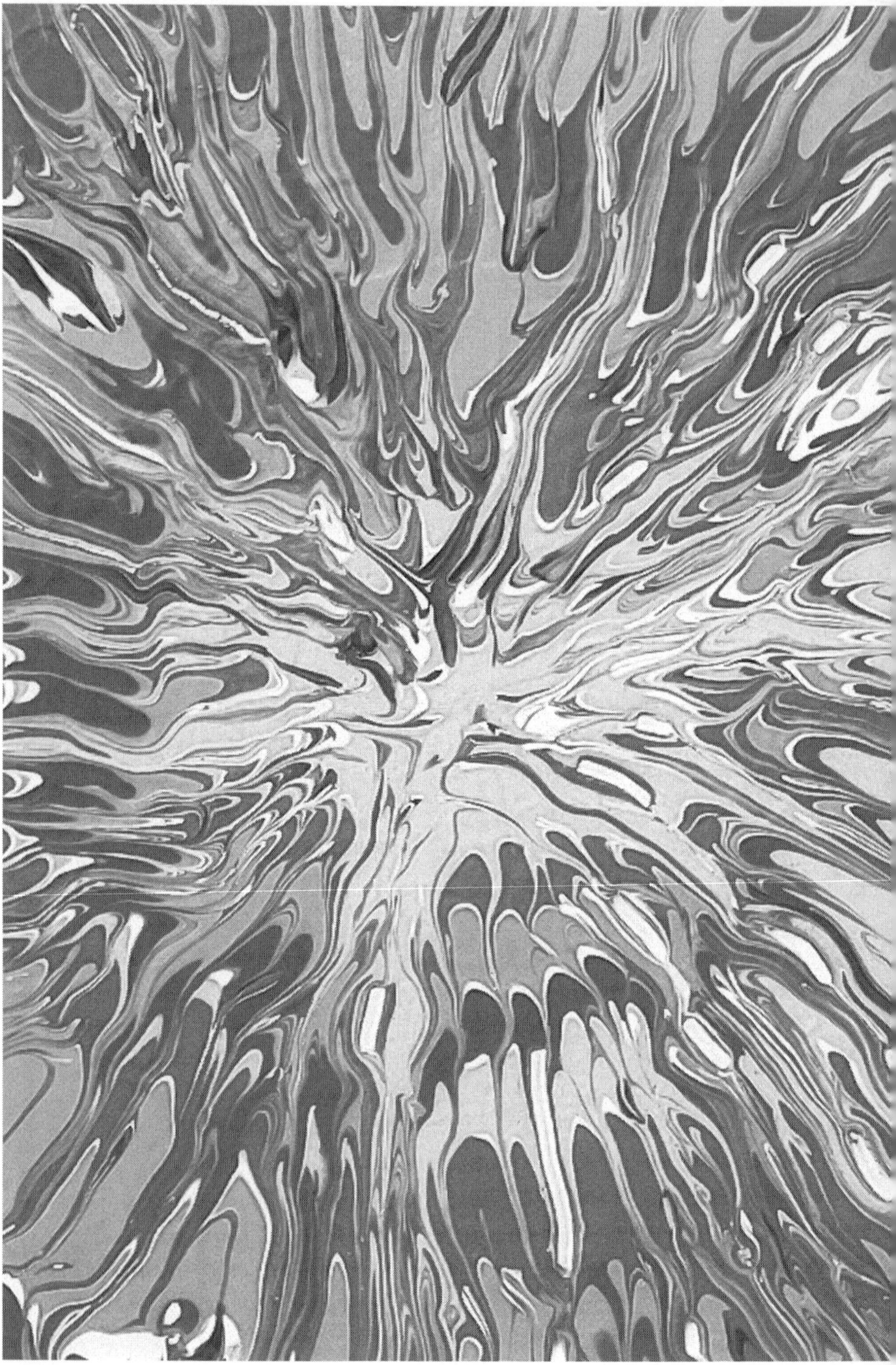

SPIRALLING THOUGHTS

I wish there was a noise loud enough to drown
these echoes of you.

FRAGMENTS

If you leave, you will carry away pieces of me.
I wonder how I will survive with all those holes
in my soul.

ALCHEMIST

Let us turn everything we touch into gold.
Together, let us elevate the world.

INNER CHILD

You appeal to the 15-year-old me.
She did not know heartbreak yet.
When I met you I met her again.
Here she is, ready to put her all into this,
with an abandon that
only the naïve are capable of.

CUSTOM-MADE

Bask in my love for you.
It is your very own private Sun.

7.83 Hz

I have listened to your heartbeat.
There is nothing else I need to hear.
There can be no greater truth.

DRIFTERS

Today when the whole world seems to do our bidding,
there's still something that refuses to listen –
the human heart.
It is still delightfully bohemian.

YOU SOLVED MY JIGSAW

I lost an important piece of myself as I went through life.
It was always out there, waiting for the time
when I was ready to be complete again.
Meeting you has put me together.
Knowing you has given me peace.

I STAKE NO CLAIM

I tried to claim your love through cliches.
But now I know better.
Your love is the Cosmos and I exist in it.
Your love houses me.

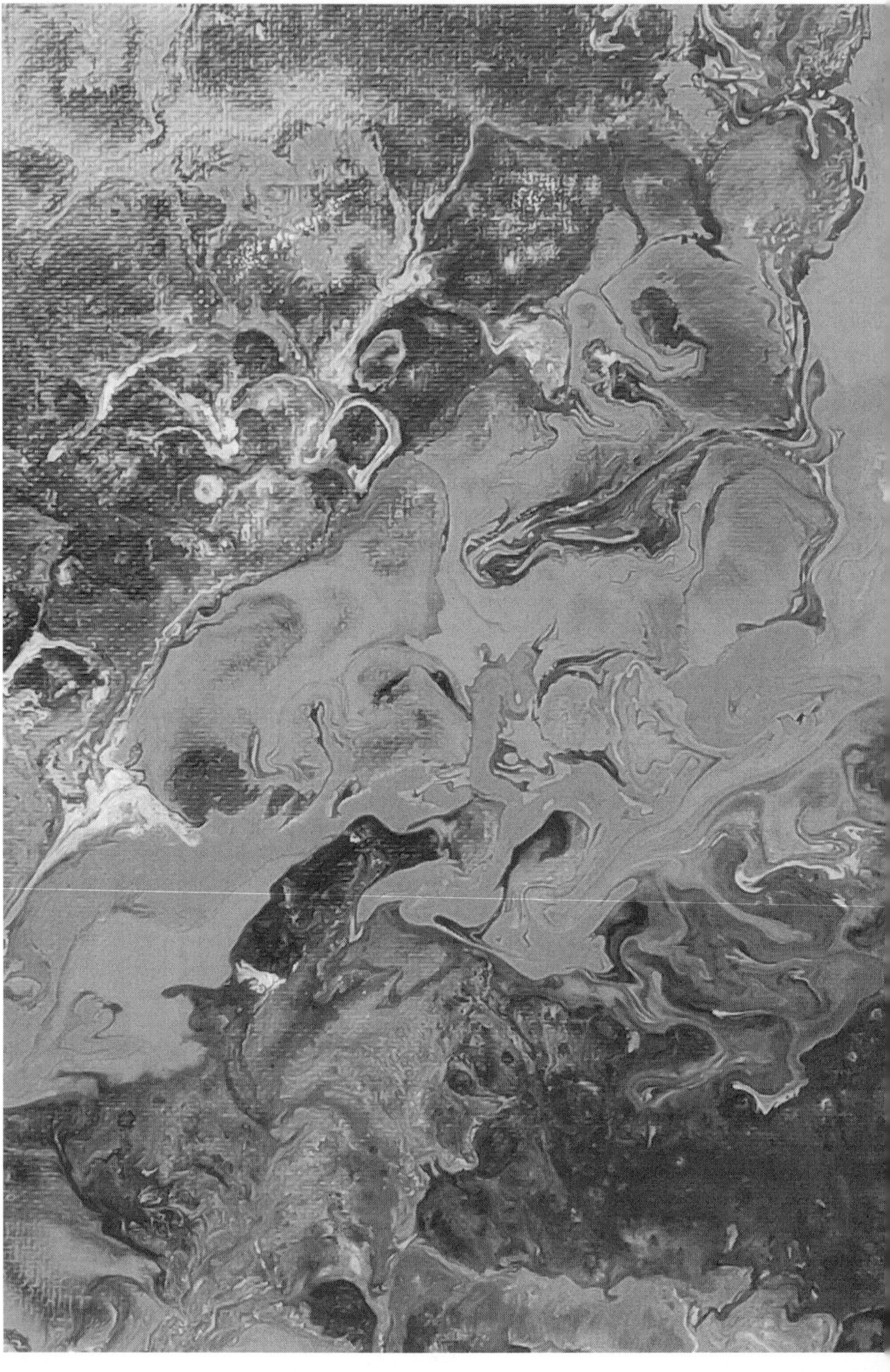

CONDEMNED

You are the smudge on my soul.
You are my guilty pleasure.

FERAL

This thing I feel for you is so powerful
that it scares me.
I am afraid that if I allow it to run wild,
it will destroy our worlds.
And if I keep it tamed, it will destroy me.
Does that thing you feel for me scare you too?

HUMBUG

My feelings don't listen to my life's philosophies.

DIVINE

You held me with your many hands
One caressing my cheek, another holding me close
One on the small of my back, yet another moving my hair out of the way.
I am surprised to find myself alive after witnessing your *Virat Roop*.
They say mere mortals cannot survive that.

MEMORIES ARE LIKE TATTOOS

You say that I should forget all the memories
we have made.
As if I could.
As if you could.

EXQUISITE YOU

You are celestial.
I wonder how this cosmos can stay
so unaffected by you.
Why isn't there a grand celebration
of your presence in this Universe?

DNA OF THE UNIVERSE

Love is the DNA with which all universes
are built –
those in which we exist, and those that exist in us.
Love is the Space that connects everything.
Love is the common thread.

PERPLEXITIES

Why do boundaries seem so blurred?
Why can't my heart and mind agree
with each other?
Together, you and I will find a way.
And that scares me the most.

FOREVER POSTPONED

'We' exist somewhere in the future.

MY SPIRIT IS MORE AUDACIOUS THAN MY BODY

You may not feel my arms around you,
but those clouds and feathers you fly through
in your dreams?
They are me.
All me.

PREDICAMENT

May be one day we will arrive at a fork,
and both of us will choose a different tine.
This road, however beautiful, will be lonely
without you.
Sometimes a beautiful dream does turn into a nightmare.
Sometimes we only have ourselves to blame for it.

COSMIC LOVE

Our love is about galaxies, stars, planets,
and moons.
It is also about umbrae and black holes.
Our love is about everything.
Our love is about nothing.

THE DECISION THAT SURVIVED REINCARNATION

In my life you aren't coincidental.
You are a conscious, thought-through decision.

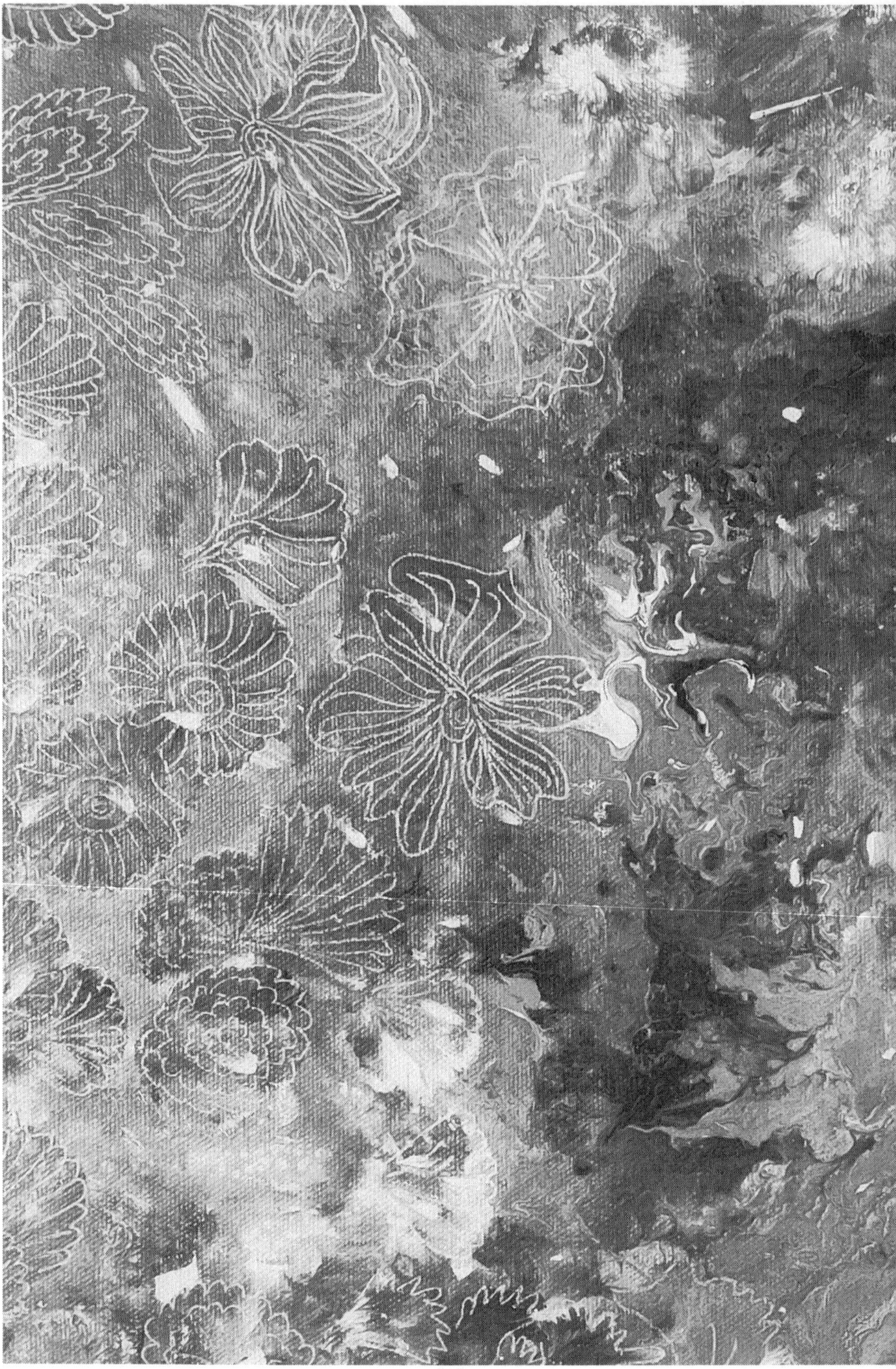

POSSESSED

I lie flat on my back
spread-eagled
life seeps through my pores
mingles with the earth
around me, saplings raise their heads,
and wither

I count seconds with my heartbeats
blood coagulates, breath freezes
it hangs in the air above my face
posing existential questions

The mind empties
one memory at a time, one thought at a time
until nothing remains
but your words, in what had once been
my brain.

SURVIVORS

Through our fights, disappointments, and silences,
there's one thing that has stayed unchanged –
my determination to go on loving you.
This gives me more faith in us than anything else.

WITHOUT YOU, I AM RADIOACTIVE

With all the wars that electrons and protons
keep waging on each other,
it is a miracle that atoms do not explode.
And, yet, you ask why loving you
is so important to me.

NESTED LIVES

With you each moment is a lifetime.
Every time I dig through these moments,
I pull out a different interpretation
to daydream about.

CATHARSIS

I didn't know I was capable of feeling
something this intense.
You brought me back to life.
You made me believe in myself.

TIME TOO HAS TATTOOS

When there are such few memories to cherish,
all our moments need to be deeply engraved
in time.
So I keep replaying them in my mind.

LOVE FOR THE INDIAN SOUL

Ordinary love can hardly be an inspiration.
For poetry to emerge, love needs some spices.
I have loved you for a long time now.
Thank you for adding the *tadka*.

FIRE IS EASIER ON THE SKIN THAN WATER

Your love is making me walk the fire.
But I would rather burn on the cinders
than drown in the numbness
of a life without you.

FLYING IN LOVE

I have never been more in love.
I have never been more free.

WABI-SABI

The moments we had,
and the ones we lost,
define our bond
And our bond is beautiful,
if not perfect.

MILESTONES

For decades, passers-by indulged my incoherence.
When you came along, I found the thread.
I learnt how to talk.

CHECKS AND BALANCES

Loving you is the hardest thing I have ever done.
It gives me the worst kind of sorrow.
And yet I prefer to go on loving you.
Because loving you is the easiest thing
I have ever done.
It gives me the best kind of happiness too.

I ENVY YOU

Few people are lucky enough
to have someone feel for them the way
I feel for you.
Treasure this. It is rare.

DREAMING OF A LONG DRIVE

I love driving alone.
With the music turned on loud.
Singing along my favourite songs.
Cruising along smooth, straight roads.
But every now and then, I am surprised to find my palm
pressed on the empty seat beside me and my heart wishing
that you could materialize there.
If that could happen, maybe we could talk.
And never stop.

I AM BUT A MEDIUM

Have you noticed the stars shining in my eyes
when I look at you?
That is nothing but the Universe
channelling its love for you.

WE ARE HOMOGENEOUS

That day when we first held hands, I felt
our souls merge.
That moment was infinite. We were infinite.
Whenever we are apart, that infinity
embraces me.
I still feel your hand in mine.
I still find your soul in me.

THE SUN RISES

Darkness starts descending as soon as you leave.
Swallowing cities, silencing creatures,
it slithers up my body.
But then you rise again.
No darkness, however powerful,
can survive your presence.

SPECTRAL RADIO

I lose my ability to talk whenever you are around.
But my heart is quite talkative
when it comes to
having silent conversations with you.
You just need to find the right frequency
and tune in to it.

A WORTHY JOURNEY

With you, I have the patience.
I want to wait and see where this goes.
With you, I know that the future will one day
respond to all these years of yearning.
Or maybe it will not.
With you, I know each experience will be beautiful
even if it brings pain.

ESTUARY

Let's meet tomorrow.
You bring your calm. I'll get my chaos.
I might ruffle your surface a bit,
but your calm will triumph.
My chaos will be calmed.
This is ancient wisdom. Who am I to argue with it?

GRAVITY

Years ago, I wandered into an orbit around you.
I began each revolution fearing that it may be my last.
Because when I am out there, at the far edge of your solar system,
I feel your pull slacken.
I find myself wondering whether I am necessary to your world.
If I choose to slink off, would you know that I am gone?
There are bands of maverick comets wrecking a havoc in the Universe.
I glance at them and
continue my orbit.
I want to see you one last time.
This time may be, you will tell me
that you've missed me too.

HAPPY ENDING

Your eyes led me away.
Else, I was staring at a world
devastated by the fire
of the absence of your love.

I was aghast that such a world could exist
where I would need to survive, being aware
that I could have been in your arms
but I chose to let you go.

Instead, the scared me skirted the fire,
and let our fingers entwine.
Now, we make our way ahead,
your hands exploring me,
your ravenous mouth whispering words
guiding flowers to bloom and birds to sing.

While we create our cacophonous music,
and stitch our erratic story,
I sometimes look back at the fire.
Was it a friend or a foe? If I had chosen
to go through it, would I have emerged
shining like purified gold?

Would this golden me have then waited
for my afraid being to drag the rotting carcass of a cursed love,
to the same end, and then shared the wisdom—
"There never was a happy ending to this?"